gr♥w

BIBLE STUDY
for
Committed ∧ Couples
UNMARRIED

Natasha Jo Benevides

INKY FLOCK PRESS
TORONTO | CANADA

ACKNOWLEDGEMENTS:

This project involved a number of people,
who generously gave of their time and talent
to bring it to fruition:

The Doerksens of Woodland Associates
Nathan Allen of Nathan Allen Studios
Joel Benevides
Melody & Darren Zammit
Chenoa Hill

ADDITIONAL THANKS
for consultation & guidance from:

Neil Josephson – Family Life Canada
Stephen Sheane – Bramalea Baptist Church
Dean Kennedy – Nashville Road Community Church

SCRIPTURE QUOTES:

Multiple versions of scripture were used in this work
(including video sessions), accessed online from
www.biblegateway.com

Published by Inky Flock Press
Toronto, Ontario, Canada

ISBN: 978-1-9994628-1-9

CONTENTS

INTRODUCTION

GROW Bible Study for Committed Unmarried Couples is NOT a pre-marital training course. If you are engaged and looking for those materials, check with Christian resources online, or contact your local church.

Although the biblical value of marriage is timeless, Pastor Natasha recognizes that not everyone is at the place in their relationship where they are ready to make this life-long commitment.

Each of the four sessions has five parts: the video session with a follow along page in your workbook, a candid *Share* from Pastor Natasha, a *Time to Get Real* challenge for you and your partner, *The Story Continues* with further sharing, and a *Walk the Talk* session for you and your partner to work through.

For maximum benefit, each session should be completed weekly (including homework). At the most, this study should be wrapped up within six to eight weeks.

This workbook is specifically designed for one per person so you can take and share your notes, and is to go with the GROW video sessions, which can be found at:

Scan QR code with your phone. If it doesn't work, videos can by found on the author's Youtube channel: Natasha Jo Benevides, under Playlists, Grow Bible Study

SESSION 1

IDENTITY IN CHRIST

" '...^{37}Love the Lord your God with all your heart and with all your soul and with all your mind.' ^{38}This is the first and greatest commandment. ^{39}And the second is like it: 'Love your neighbor as yourself.' ^{40}All the law and the prophets hang on these two commandments." – JESUS speaking in Matthew 22:37-40

VIDEO NOTES

This four session course is designed to help you grow in your understanding of:

Your _____ in Christ

Your _____ with your partner

Your _____ with God

The foundation for this study is based on Matthew _____, which reads:

"Love the Lord your _____ with all your _____ and with all your _____ and with all your _____. This is the first and greatest commandment. And the second is like it: _____ your neighbor as yourself. All the law and the prophets _____ _____ these two commandments."

Of the four different kinds of love written about in the Bible, the fourth kind is called _____ love.

God loves us deeply and passionately because of Who our _____ is grounded in.

"Jesus came to announce to us that an identity based on success, popularity and power is a false identity - an illusion! Loudly and clearly he says: 'You are not what the world makes you; but you are children of God.'" - Henri J.M. Nouwen, *Here and Now: Living in the Spirit*

SHARE: IDENTITY CRISIS

For the first half of my life, I didn't know Jesus. I had heard of Him, but just assumed He was some ancient sage who spouted enough wisdom to result in a bunch of misguided people making Him out to be God instead of just a really cool human.

Not knowing Jesus meant I didn't have to play by His rules. I could do what I wanted, act the way I wanted and leave my morals in the dust. So I did just that. All my grandstanding and strutting was intended to create the image of what the world defined as a modern, liberated woman. It was really just a front though. It was like I had built a set to stage my life on, but the hidden parts, the framework, were made of rotting lumber.

I often found myself angry and depressed. I kept looking for that perfect guy, that perfect relationship...the one I had been groomed to expect as my happily-ever-after through chick flicks and romance novels and social media posts by couples who were apparently madly in love. A number of whom were, in reality, struggling and on the brink of a total relationship meltdown.

Some of my guy friends have shared similar stories. Except in the male version their destiny is to get hot babes, be in a band, drive muscle cars and party every weekend.

Society told me that because I made my own choices, I was empowered...but I didn't feel powerful. I would listen to self-help 'gurus' who taught that in order to prosper all I had to do was declare it and unleash the power within. So I'd tell myself in the mirror that I was destined for great things, but my reflection just looked back and laughed, saying, *you may have them all fooled but **I know the real you.***

Does any of this sound familiar?

TIME TO GET REAL

From the list below, put an **X** beside the ***positive*** qualities you want other people to believe about you, and then an **O** beside the qualities you believe about yourself.

- Smart
- Fun to be around
- Attractive
- Confident
- Brave
- Down to Earth
- Humble
- Caring
- Thoughtful
- Happy

Now, from the list below, put an **X** beside the ***negative*** qualities you think other people believe about you, and then an **O** beside the qualities you believe about yourself.

- Angry
- Critical
- Unattractive
- Fearful
- Selfish
- Deceitful
- Arrogant
- Boring
- Stubborn
- Cynical

DISCUSS: What did you notice? Share with your partner.

THE STORY CONTINUES: A NEW CREATION

Cynicism is definitely one of my most lingering negative qualities. When I hear a speech from a politician, I typically assume he or she is lying. When I see a commercial selling wrinkle cream I snort at their shot of a nineteen-year-old model using the product.

So when the mission to discover my true identity and worth kept leading me to the Bible, I figured it was just another *rah-rah you've had the power in you all along* cliché. But it wasn't.

It was a book that told a story. A holy story about how God created me to be this amazing person, but a seed of wickedness got into the mix, so I grew to believe that my only value was if I conformed to how the world told me I should be. I allowed the whole world to be the judge...including myself.

So, God sent His son Jesus to wash away that ugly seed and restore me to who God always intended for me to be, someone made in His image through Christ. But God wanted something from me in return.

In order to discover this identity my soul longed for, an identity that was so immersed in God's unconditional love and acceptance that I was breathing it like air, I had to believe. Not just with my mind, but believe also with my heart that Jesus is who the Bible says He is, and did what the Bible said He did:

"If anyone acknowledges that Jesus is the Son of God, God lives in them and they in God." - 1 John 4:15

"Therefore, if anyone is in Christ, the new creation has come: The old has gone, the new is here!" - 2 Corinthians 5:17

It took some time but finally I believed...oh how I believed!

And suddenly God entered into my messy life and began to affect my relationships. Especially with Joel, who I had recently married after four years of living together.

It's like there were two Natasha's. The new Natasha was fresh and unique and full of excitement over the prospect of a life connected to God. The old Natasha retreated into the dark corners of my being, knowing her time was up but determined to gnaw and jab and try to lure me back into the flatness of my life before Jesus.

Over the years, with the ever present help of the Bible, the Holy Spirit, and other Christians, my identity in Christ has grown. It continues to be a lifelong process of wrestling though. Wrestling against the voice that tells me I'm failing, I'm not good enough, I'll never be happy...but I know unequivocally that voice is not the voice of God. And if it's not the voice of God, it's lying.

How do I know that? Because God loves me with *Agapé* love – He is passionately invested in my well-being and growth as a Christ-follower and would never steer me wrong.

*If your heart's desire is to see your
relationship with your partner flourish,
it must start with understanding your identity
as being one whose very existence is based on
receiving and sharing the selfless love
of God given through Jesus.*

WALK THE TALK

1) Over the next week, research online "Bible verses about identity." Choose two that are meaningful to you and write them below:

a) _____
   _____
   _____
   _____

b) _____
   _____
   _____
   _____

What is it about these two verses that impacted you?

_____
_____
_____
_____

DISCUSS: Share with your partner and talk about
anything new you may have learned
about yourself or God.

2) Not all couples move at the same pace in their spiritual journey. Some are in the 'discovery' stage and are still processing the incredible heart of the Creator, found in the biblical passage:

John 3:16 "For God so loved the world, that he gave his only son [Jesus], that whoever believes in him shall not perish but have eternal life."

Others are in the 'responsive' stage where, having received God's love, they are growing in their desire to give that love back to God through building a deeper relationship with Him by surrendering selfishness:

Matthew 16:24 "Then Jesus said to his disciples, 'Whoever wants to be my disciple must deny themselves and take up their cross and follow me.'"

Many of us are somewhere in between.

Consider where you believe you're at in your spiritual journey and how that affects your personal identity. Note your thoughts below and compare your answers with your partner's:

_____

_____

_____

_____

_____

_____

3) Taking into account your answers and discussion (in both the *TIME TO GET REAL* and *WALK THE TALK* sections), sum up in one or two sentences what you believe your combined identities say about you as a couple. Write below and share your answer with your partner:

_____

_____

_____

_____

_____

SESSION 2
AGAPE LOVE

" '...³⁷Love the Lord your God with all your heart and with all your soul and with all your mind.' ³⁸This is the first and greatest commandment. ³⁹And the second is like it: 'Love your neighbor as yourself.' ⁴⁰All the law and the prophets hang on these two command-ments.'" – JESUS speaking in Matthew 22:37-40

VIDEO NOTES

The Greek word for neighbor is _____, which means any person other than ourself. In the case of a couple, it's _____ the other.

Using the example of the Good Samaritan's selfless mercy on an injured Jew, Jesus said we are are to _____ and do _____.

The Oxford dictionary defines mercy as: "...showing _____ or _____ toward one whom we have the power to punish or harm."

With *Agapé* love we're _____, regardless of whether or not we believe our partner deserves it.

Our goal is to help our partner _____, not to defend ourselves or be _____.

The truth is your partner may not recognize when you're extending _____ toward him or her.

Galatians 5:13 states that we are to "_____ one another in love."

"...when the story of earth is told, all that will be remembered is the truth we exchanged. The vulnerable moments. The terrifying risk of love and the care we took to cultivate it. And all the rest, the distracting noises of insecurity and the flattery and the flashbulbs will flicker out like a turned-off television."
— Donald Miller, *Scary Close: Dropping the Act and Acquiring a Taste for True Intimacy*

SHARE: TO TELL THE TRUTH

When people feel offended or put off by another's behavior or comments, they react in different ways. Some call it out immediately, some brood or sulk, and some have the astounding ability to simply let it go.

I am a seether. When Joel and I first started living together, I'd put up a great façade in my attempts to portray what I thought was the perfect mate. I would watch sports with him and do all the cooking and try to keep our home to a standard that met his expectations...but oh I stewed about it.

And because I wasn't being truthful about who I was or how I saw things, inevitably the internal pressure would build and we would have a no-holds-barred couple's throwdown.

The funny thing was, once I became a follower of Jesus shortly after we married I found myself *wanting* to do things to bless Joel. Although to this day I don't enjoy cooking (nope...never will) I began to willingly make meals that I knew he liked. I became more attuned to him and found joy in showing him God's love through simple acts.

In a bizarre twist, it totally weirded Joel out. I was no longer the fiery party girl who pretended to be agreeable and then lunged at the chance to tear him down. His volatile playmate had vanished before his eyes and he was left with...*gulp*...a wife.

This was too much for him. He decided that he needed some space and announced that we should separate. Now, the old me would have said "see ya!" and been out the door. This was my default mode for self-preservation. But the new me understood the *consequences* of this split – for Joel, for my two daughters, for me. More brokenness.

So I chose to do something different. Something I hadn't done before when it came to confrontation. I chose to follow the biblical example of telling the truth in love.

Ephesians 4:15 - "Instead, speaking the truth in love, we will grow to become in every respect the mature body of him who is the head, that is, Christ."

Ephesians 4:25 - "Therefore each of you must put off falsehood and speak truthfully to your neighbor [or 'other']..."

God calls us to be honest with one another, but He doesn't want us to be mean about it. When we tell the truth in love, we are more concerned about the other person's well-being than our own. We are practicing *Agapé* love.

I told Joel that I didn't want to split up as we had made a covenant before God. However, I also made it clear to him that if he left me because of my faith, according to scripture I was no longer bound to him and could decide to move on. I wanted to make sure he was completely clear on the potential consequences of his actions:

1 Corinthians 7:12-15 – "12 To the rest I say this (I, not the Lord): If any brother has a wife who is not a believer and she is willing to live with him, he must not divorce her. 13 And if a woman has a husband who is not a believer and he is willing to live with her, she must not divorce him. 14 For the unbelieving husband has been sanctified through his wife, and the unbelieving wife has been sanctified through her believing husband. Otherwise your children would be unclean, but as it is, they are holy. 15 But if the unbeliever leaves, let it be so. The brother or the sister is not bound in such circumstances; God has called us to live in peace."

Telling your partner a truth they don't want to hear can be painful for both of you. But telling it in love instead of using it as a weapon to tear him or her down can lead to something miraculous – growth.

TIME TO GET REAL

In order to learn how to tell the truth in love, you must first ask the Holy Spirit to reveal any bitterness or resentment you are harboring toward your partner.

1) Take a <u>minimum</u> of fifteen minutes to spend before God alone, and...

- Ask Him to show you any anger or grudges you are holding against your partner. Note whatever comes to mind here:

_____

_____

_____

_____

2) Ask God's forgiveness for judging another when He alone is the judge:

James 4:12 – *"There is only one Lawgiver and Judge, the one who is able to save and destroy. But you - who are you to judge your neighbor?"*

3) What is your greatest desire for your partner? (*HINT!* remember it's not about you) What blessings do you hope to see God bestow upon him or her? Jot down your answers here:

_____

_____

_____

_____

4) Go to your partner and...
- confess what you've been holding a grudge about (*HINT!* speak without accusation; and listen without lashing out)
- ask for your partner's forgiveness; and forgive your partner in turn
- share what your greatest desire for his or her life is

THE STORY CONTINUES: LOVE LOVE LOVE

In the first video session you were introduced to the concept of different types of love, with *Agapé* being the one that is self-sacrificial and wholly concerned with the well-being of another.

Let's face it though, expecting to remain in this perfect state of always loving others selflessly is unrealistic. As followers of Jesus, we are works in progress and so sometimes settle for the less demanding favorite-old-slipper feel of *Phileō* love –

that is the companionable best friends kind of love. Which works great when things are going well, but doesn't have the power to endure the deeper (and sometimes rougher) waters of committed relationships for any extended period.

The story of the apostle Peter is fairly well known. As one of the twelve disciples, he passionately and repeatedly swore his allegiance to Jesus...only to completely abandon Him when He was arrested. While Jesus was spit upon, beaten and scourged, Peter was busy shaking his head and insisting he didn't know the guy.

But when Jesus was crucified, Peter was completely consumed by guilt. He was deeply ashamed and horrified that he had placed his own need for self-preservation above standing for the God-man he had faithfully followed 24/7 for three incredible years.

So, when Jesus rose from the dead and once again walked among them, He sought Peter out with the specific intention of extending forgiveness.

Peter, head hung low, hears his Lord ask in John 21:15 "...Simon [Peter] son of John, do you love me...?"

Peter would have not heard the English word "love" like our translation, but instead he heard "*Agapé*" or an Aramaic term that would have conveyed a similar depth of selfless commitment.

There was no mistaking Jesus' question. In fact, He said it three times just so that His disgraced disciple clearly understood that he was being asked to put Jesus first once and for all. Ah, but Peter...you gotta smile.

Ashamed, sorrowful, guilt-ridden Peter, who is given this wonderful shot at restoration, chooses to answer with, "you know I love you Lord." But it's *Phileō* love! It's like he was saying, "yup, I know you want me to offer you this holy sacrificial you-first kind of love...but let's settle for the fact that I love you like a best friend? Sound good?"

And guess what? Although that is *not* an acceptable choice when it comes to the relationship we have with our Creator, in our relationship with our human partner, at times it really *is* okay. At times that's all we may need or have to give.

When Joel wanted to separate because of my faith and I told him I'd then consider myself no longer obligated to remain married, it gave him pause. He thought about it and then decided we should stay together. I would love to tell you what a good little Christian I was in my bliss of this happy news, but I'd be flat out lying.

Joel and I were raised in dysfunction. And as adults we continued the cycle in our own dysfunctional relationships. The word dysfunction should have been included in our wedding vows...seriously. It was true what I'd told him earlier – that I didn't want us to break up, but there was also a part of me that no longer wanted to be committed to a man who didn't share my faith.

If we stayed together I just *knew* it was going to be hard. And I wasn't wrong. Joel was doing stuff behind my back that was dishonoring to me and our marriage. When I tried to talk to him about a sermon I'd heard or prayer answered he was dismissive. When I gave money to the church he would become offended and argumentative.

So why did I stay? Because I believed that God was urging me to love Joel through it, to be more concerned for my partner's ultimate well-being than the temporary season of persecution I was living out.

In all of it though my heart's desire wasn't for Joel to love me back with that same sacrificial kind of love. What I was actually longing for was a beloved companion, a best friend who would journey alongside me in the extraordinary life I now had in Jesus. I was hungering for *Phileō* love.

WALK THE TALK

1) Think about your partner's well-being. In life, work, health, family. List 3 things that you are not already doing but can start to do to contribute to your partner's positive growth:

_____
_____
_____
_____

2) How do you think *Agapé* love (flowing from God, out of you, toward your partner) is practiced in your relationship?

_____
_____
_____
_____

3) Take a minimum of 10 minutes together and pray for one another. For blessings and guidance and other positive things for your partner that the Lord lays on your heart.

SESSION 3

PUTTING GOD FIRST

"...[37] Love the Lord your God with all your heart and with all your soul and with all your mind.' [38] This is the first and greatest commandment. [39] And the second is like it: 'Love your neighbor as yourself.' [40] All the law and the prophets hang on these two commandments." – JESUS speaking in Matthew 22:37-40

Jesus often quoted from the Old Testament. In this case, it came out of Deuteronomy 6:4-7, in which Moses says: "Hear O Israel: the LORD our God, the LORD is one. _____ the LORD your God will all your _____ and with all your _____ and with all your _____."

God desires for us to live a life in _____ to Him in return for the incredible love that He give to us.

God wants us to choose to enter into a loving relationship with Him. He _____ to force human beings to love Him back.

Following Jesus is not easy. We are called to _____ to our selfish ways in order to _____ in Him. We have to surrender control of our lifestyle, our choices, and even our _____.

God calls us to love Him first, before others or ourselves. He is our Creator and will not settle for second place. This is our response to God giving Himself so _____ and loving us so _____.

"When I have learned to love God better than my earthly dearest, I shall love my earthly dearest better than I do now."

– C.S. Lewis

SHARE: THE TEST AND THE TRIAL

When Joel wanted to split up and then changed his mind, I didn't stay because I wanted to or even felt I had to. I took the Bible at its word when it said I was free from obligation if my unbelieving spouse chose to leave. Since he had made the choice to do so, I felt released in the sight of God.

I stayed because in a time of prayer and listening to God, He made it clear it was His desire that I stick it out. I stayed out of obedience to God. I obeyed not because I was afraid of God's wrath, but because my obedience was a way in which I could honor Him and express my love in return for His unfailing presence, grace and love toward me.

I came to realize that there was no one else – neither parents, nor partners, nor kids – who would have my absolute best interests at heart more than God did. And none who had the ability to see those best interests come to fruition the way He could. So, in complete trust, I put myself in the Lord's hands and stayed.

For quite a while, it didn't go so well. On the surface, Joel agreed to some lifestyle changes that would help us to grow closer and healthier as a couple. In secret though, nothing had changed for him...other than now he was hiding more things from me than ever before.

TIME TO GET REAL

What is your first memory of learning about God? How old were you? What was your impression of Him?

_____

_____

_____

_____

_____

What is your impression of Him now? Do you believe God loves you unconditionally? Explain why.

_____

_____

_____

_____

_____

As you share your answers with your partner, note the similarities and differences between your impressions of God and discuss:

_____

_____

_____

_____

_____

THE STORY CONTINUES: BLESSING UPON BLESSING

Despite my awareness of Joel's ongoing shenanigans and conduct, I started treating him with more honor and respect. The Holy Spirit was transforming me from the inside out, and practicing unconditional *Agapé* love toward Joel without expecting anything in return began to have an effect.

He started coming to church with me. A little freaked out and somewhat convinced that people would judge him for his long hair and tattoos (most didn't), but attending nonetheless. And then he started asking questions.

By the time I stepped into my call to work at a church, he was actually enjoying participating in worship and listening to sermons. We joined a small group together where both he and his questions were welcomed. I watched Joel transform before my eyes.

The next thing I knew, he joined the couples ministry with me, and then stepped out on his own and joined both the worship team and men's ministry.

As Joel grew in his own relationship with God, it suddenly brought a new freshness and invigoration to our marriage. This went beyond simply now having something in common. It was about moving from a mind understanding to a heart revelation of what Jesus had done for us and how that enabled us to begin the process of becoming the Joel and Natasha our Creator had always intended for us to be.

In 2009, Joel was baptized and, to my incredible delight and gratitude, our two grown daughters followed shortly thereafter.

Whenever I am going through a circumstance in which I feel

my hope starting to sputter, I remember the incredible work God did in our lives...and will continue doing. Why did He do all this? Selfless, unconditional, uncontainable, holy and glorious love.

In addition to that most famous quote from John 3:16 (*for God so loved the world*) mentioned in Session 1, the Bible has a multitude of passages that speak of God's love and provision. Here are just a handful:

John 10:10 – "The thief [devil] comes only to steal and kill and destroy; I [Jesus] have come that they may have life, and have it to the full."

Romans 8:37-39 – "^{37}No, in all these things we are more than conquerors through him who loved us. ^{38}For I am convinced that neither death nor life, neither angels nor demons, neither the present nor the future, nor any powers, ^{39}neither height nor depth, nor anything else in all creation, will be able to separate us from the love of God that is in Christ Jesus our LORD."

Zephaniah 3:17 – "The LORD your God is with you, the Mighty Warrior who saves. He will take great delight in you; in his love he will no longer rebuke you, but will rejoice over you with singing."

Galatians 2:20 – "I have been crucified with Christ and I no longer live, but Christ lives in me. The life I now live in the body, I live by faith in the Son of God, who loved me and gave himself for me."

Matthew 6:31-33 – "^{31} So do not worry, saying, 'What shall we eat?' or 'What shall we drink?' or 'What shall we wear?' ^{32} For the pagans run after all these things, and your heavenly Father knows that you need them. ^{33} But seek first his kingdom and his righteousness, and all these things will be given to you as well."

WALK THE TALK

1) Like all relationships, yours with God is two-sided. As you increase in awareness of the depths of His feelings and commitment towards you, in what ways are you responding in meeting His expectation of putting Him first?

_____

_____

_____

_____

_____

2) Very early on in scripture, God makes His people aware of how passionate and possessive He is toward us:

Exodus 34:14 – "for you shall not worship any other god, for the LORD, whose name is Jealous, is a jealous God."

Song of Solomon 8:6 – "Place me like a seal over your heart, like a seal on your arm; for love is as strong as death, its jealousy [zeal, passion, commitment] unyielding as the grave. It burns like blazing fire, like a mighty flame [like the very flame of the LORD]."

When you reflect on these passages, which clearly lay out that God's love towards you is so deep that He will absolutely not settle for second place in your life or heart, what thoughts come to mind?

_____

_____

_____

_____

_____

3) Do you believe that if you put "the Kingdom" (that is the sovereignty of God and His will for your life) first, He will meet all your needs as stated in Matthew 6:33? Why or why not?

_____

_____

_____

_____

_____

DISCUSS: Share your answers with your partner

SESSION 4

A CALL TO ACTION

" '...³⁷Love the Lord your God with all your heart and with all your soul and with all your mind.' ³⁸This is the first and greatest commandment. ³⁹And the second is like it: 'Love your neighbor as yourself.' ⁴⁰All the law and the prophets hang on these two commandments.' " – JESUS speaking in Matthew 22:37-40

VIDEO NOTES

Our journey with Jesus is always meant to be a _____ one.

How do you envision your _____ with your partner growing? Where do you _____ ____ going from here?

Marriage is not a _____ construct. It was _____ by God.

Other earthly creatures weren't created in the _____ of God. Only humans were (as both spiritual and physical beings), and that sets us apart.

As a result, sex for humans is not merely a physical act. It brings in a _____ element so powerful that it is meant to come under the _____ of marriage.

Real, genuine, unconditional *Agapé* love is _____ important to God.

1 Corinthians 13:1 reads... "If I speak in the tongues of men and of angels, but have not _____, I am only a resounding gong or clanging symbol [shallow, empty, hollow]."

"For all its peculiarities and unevenness, the Bible has a simple story. God made man [that is: humans]. Man rejected God. God won't give up until he wins him back. God will whisper. He will shout. He will touch and tug. He will take away our burdens; he'll even take away our blessings. If there are a thousand steps between us and him, he will take all but one. But he will leave the final one for us. The choice is ours." – Max Lucado, *Grace for the Moment: Inspirational Thoughts for Each Day of the Year*

SHARE: FORWARD FLAWED

I'm a hypocrite. I judge others in the blink of an eye and go on junk food binges and covet things I don't really need. I am in a constant ebb and flow of doing great in my journey with God and then stumbling along until I fall on my knees in a prayer of confession and humility. I am – as all Christians are – a work in progress.

But the point is that I *progress*.

When Joel and I argue or come up against each other, we're not even in the same stratosphere of rage and frustration as we were before God entered into our relationship.

We rarely fight, we often pray, and despite some continued valleys of pain we've had to go through (stories for another time), we've come out closer and stronger.

Don't get me wrong, our relationship is far from perfect. But with God's help, it has become perfect for us.

TIME TO GET REAL

1) Reflect on your relationship with your partner from the time you've been together until now.

   List three areas of improvement as a couple:

   _____

   _____

   _____

   List three areas you're still struggling in:

   _____

   _____

   _____

2) In the video session, you were asked if you believed you were capable of putting your partner's best interests ahead of your own. Do you? Why or why not?

   _____

   _____

   _____

   _____

   DISCUSS: Share your answers with your partner.

THE STORY CONTINUES: FINAL THOUGHTS

In this study, you looked at who you are in Christ, how you can be lovingly selfless toward your partner, and what God's desire and expectation of you is in your relationship with Him. Finally, you have been challenged to consider where you and your partner are headed moving forward.

Let me be clear, you *do not* have to get married. But if that sacred union which invites the Creator into your committed relationship is not your mutual destination, then what is?

Speaking of destinations, as followers of Jesus we believe that there is an eternal, joyous life beyond this one. A life as our fully realized selves in the presence of a wondrous God more incredible than we can even imagine:

Psalm 16:11 – "You make know to me the path of life; you will fill me with joy in your presence, with eternal pleasures at your right hand."

Though our relationship with God is forever, marriage *isn't*. It doesn't cross the threshold from this world into the next:

Mark 12:25 – "[Jesus said] When the dead rise, they will neither marry nor be given in marriage; they will be like the angels in heaven."

Knowing that the man that I've come to love so deeply and am journeying with side-by-side in this life with will one day no longer belong to me makes our marriage and time together infinitely more precious.

When we were living together, there was a part of me that (because of my own dysfunction) was not only expecting Joel to fail as my other, but had some twisted inner drive to push him toward that precipice.

Now I'm all in. Joel's all in. And God? Well, He was *always* all in. Your call. Your choice. Either way...be blessed friend.

WALK THE TALK

1) Where would you would like to see yourselves as a couple in one, three and five years from now? Describe below:

_____

_____

_____

_____

2) Do you believe you and your partner are the right fit (*not perfect...doesn't exist!*) for each other? Why or why not?

_____

_____

_____

_____

3) 2 Timothy 1:7 tells us God did not give us a spirit of fear or confusion. If you are either staying with your partner or not moving forward out of fear of being alone or making a mistake, how can you overcome that with God's help?

_____

_____

_____

_____

DISCUSS: Share your answers with your partner.

ADDITIONAL RESOURCES

BOOKS:

The Five Love Languages by Dr. Gary Chapman

Things I Wish I'd Known Before We Got Married by Dr. Gary Chapman

Love & Respect: The Love She Most Desires, the Respect He Desperately Needs by Dr. Emerson Eggerichs

The Total Money Makeover by Dave Ramsey

Marriage vs. Living Together – 10 Reasons to Take the Plunge! by Natasha Benevides

ONLINE:

Family Life Canada – www.familylifecanada.com

Family Life USA – www.familylife.com

Prepare Enrich Couples Check Up – www.enrichcanada.ca

Discover God's Purpose for You – www.freeshapetest.com

Made in United States
Orlando, FL
05 May 2025

61034628R00022